MOUNT RUSHMORE

by Susan Rose Simms

Cody Koala

An Imprint of Pop!
popbooksonline.com

J978.3

abdopublishing.com
Published by Pop!, a division of ABDO, PO Box 398166, Minneapolis,
Minnesota 55439. Copyright © 2019 by POP, LLC. International copyrights
reserved in all countries. No part of this book may be reproduced in any
form without written permission from the publisher. Pop!™ is a trademark
and logo of POP, LLC.

Printed in the United States of America, North Mankato, Minnesota

042018
092018

THIS BOOK CONTAINS
RECYCLED MATERIALS

Cover Photo: Shutterstock Images
Interior Photos: Shutterstock Images, 1, 5, 6, 9, 10, 13, 15 (top), 15 (bottom), 16,
17, 19, 21

Editor: Meg Gaertner
Series Designer: Laura Mitchell

Library of Congress Control Number: 2017963475
Publisher's Cataloging-in-Publication Data
Names: Simms, Susan Rose, author.
Title: Mount Rushmore / by Susan Rose Simms.
Description: Minneapolis, Minnesota : Pop!, 2019. | Series: US symbols |
    Includes online resources and index.
Identifiers: ISBN 9781532160462 (lib.bdg.) | ISBN 9781532161582 (ebook) |
Subjects: LCSH: Mount Rushmore National Memorial (S.D.)--Juvenile
    literature. | National monuments--Juvenile literature. | Emblems,
    National--Juvenile literature.
Classification: DDC 929.9--dc23

Hello! My name is
Cody Koala

Pop open this book and you'll find QR codes like this one, loaded with information, so you can learn even more!

Scan this code* and others like it while you read,

or visit the website below to make this book pop.

popbooksonline.com/mount-rushmore

*Scanning QR codes requires a web-enabled smart device with a QR code reader app and a camera.

Table of Contents

Chapter 1
Mount Rushmore. 4

Chapter 2
History. 8

Chapter 3
The Four Faces 14

Chapter 4
Standing Proud 18

Making Connections 22
Glossary. 23
Index 24
Online Resources 24

Mount Rushmore

The faces of four presidents look out from Mount Rushmore. They were **carved** into the rock many years ago.

Each face is the size of a six-story building.

Watch a video here!

Mount Rushmore is in the Black Hills of South Dakota. The monument was meant to **represent** America, freedom, and **democracy**.

Chapter 2

History

The Black Hills belonged to the Lakota Indians. But the US government took the land when it discovered gold in the area.

Learn more here!

GUTZON BORGLUM
SCULPTURED BY HIS SON
LINCOLN BORGLUM

Gutzon Borglum was the sculptor of the monument. He wanted Mount Rushmore to show the first 150 years of US history.

Workers began carving after the four faces were chosen. They used **dynamite** to blow up the rock. Then they drilled and **chiseled** the faces into the mountain.

It took hundreds of workers more than six years to carve the faces.

Chapter 3

The Four Faces

George Washington is the far left face. He was the first US president. Thomas Jefferson is next. He helped the country grow.

George Washington

Complete an activity here!

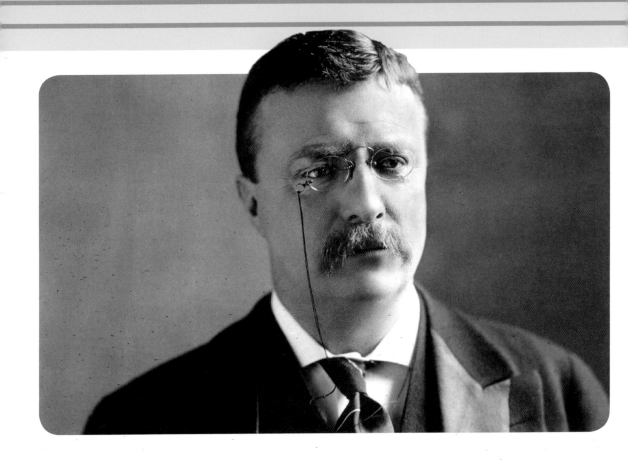

Theodore Roosevelt is
third. He helped the country
become a world leader.

Abraham Lincoln is on the far right. He held the country together during its **Civil War**.

Chapter 4

Standing Proud

Visitors walk under the flags of all 50 US states on their way to Mount Rushmore. People from all over the world come to see the four presidents.

Learn more here!

Mount Rushmore does not represent the American Indians whose land was taken. But the monument does show the United States can be a welcoming place for all people.

The head of George Washington is finished.

Abraham Lincoln's head is finished.

Carving on Mount Rushmore is complete.

1930

1937

1941

1927

1936

1939

Carving begins on the mountain.

Theodore Roosevelt's head is finished.

Thomas Jefferson's head is finished.

Making Connections

Text-to-Self

If you could choose someone to be carved on a mountain, who would you choose and why?

Text-to-Text

What other US symbols have you read about? What do they stand for?

Text-to-World

Why does it matter that the government took land from the Lakota Indians?

Glossary

carve – to cut shapes out of wood, stone, or other material.

chisel – to use a hammer and a sharp-edged tool to carefully carve into rock.

Civil War – a war between the North and the South of the United States.

democracy – a type of government that has been elected by the people.

dynamite – a powerful explosive that can blast away rock.

represent – to stand or speak for something else.

Index

Black Hills, 7, 8

Borglum, Gutzon, 11

government, 8, 20

Jefferson, Thomas, 14

Lakota Indians, 8, 20

Lincoln, Abraham, 17

president, 4, 14, 18

Roosevelt, Theodore, 16

Washington, George, 14

Online Resources

popbooksonline.com

Thanks for reading this Cody Koala book!

Scan this code* and others like it in this book, or visit the website below to make this book pop!

popbooksonline.com/mount-rushmore

*Scanning QR codes requires a web-enabled smart device with a QR code reader app and a camera.